ELEMENTS OF
LIFE

CARBON

NANCY DICKMANN

PowerKiDS
press™

Published in 2019 by **The Rosen Publishing Group, Inc.**
29 East 21st Street, New York, NY 10010

Cataloging-in-Publication Data
Names: Dickmann, Nancy.
Title: Carbon / Nancy Dickmann.
Description: New York : PowerKids Press, 2019. | Series: Elements of life | Includes glossary and index.
Identifiers: ISBN 9781538347577 (pbk.) | ISBN 9781538347591 (library bound) | ISBN 9781538347584 (6pack)
Subjects: LCSH: Carbon--Juvenile literature. | Carbon--Properties--Juvenile literature. | Chemistry, Organic--Juvenile literature. |
Group 14 elements--Juvenile literature.
Classification: LCC QD181.C1 D53 2019 | DDC 547--dc23

For Brown Bear Books Ltd:
Text and Editor: Nancy Dickmann
Designer and Illustrator: Supriya Sahai
Design Manager: Keith Davis
Picture Manager: Sophie Mortimer
Editorial Director: Lindsey Lowe
Children's Publisher: Anne O'Daly

Concept development: Square and Circus/Brown Bear Books Ltd

Picture Credits
Front Cover: Artwork, Supriya Sahai.
Interior: 123rf: molekuul, 6, photowiz, 25cr; iStock: JJ Farquitectos, 5, MW Haskin, 9, inhauscreative, 25t, Monkey Business
Images, 17r, 29b, Peopleimages, 14, Anna Shepulova, 15b, Westersoe, 23; Shutterstock: Olesia Bilkei, 17l, blurAZ, 15, Vladislav
Gajic, 25b, Matt Gertson, 19, Glenda, 12, Joe Gough, 24, Unal M. Oxmen, 8, 28, Raimundo79, 18, Kamon Saejueng, 6–7, 29t,
Zelfit, 7.
Key: t=top, b=bottom, c=center, l=left, r=right

Brown Bear Books have made every attempt to contact the copyright holders. If you have any information please contact
licensing@brownbearbooks.co.uk

Manufactured in the United States of America

CPSIA Compliance Information: Batch CWPK19: For Further Information contact Rosen Publishing, New York, New York at 1-800-237-9932

CONTENTS

ELEMENTS ALL AROUND US

Everything in the universe is made up of elements. These are basic substances that cannot be broken down into other substances. Oxygen, carbon, hydrogen, nitrogen, phosphorus, and sulfur are the most important elements for life.

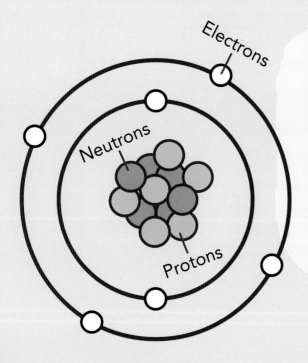

Electrons

Neutrons

Protons

IT'S ATOMIC!

The smallest unit of an element is an atom. Atoms are much too small to see. They are made up of even smaller particles called protons, neutrons, and electrons. Neutrons and protons are in the nucleus at the center of the atom. Electrons circle around the nucleus. A carbon atom has 6 protons and 6 electrons. Most have 6 neutrons, but some have 7 or 8.

Natural or Not?

About 94 elements are found in nature. Others have been made in laboratories.

COMPOUNDS

Atoms of one element can join together with atoms of another element. They form a compound, which might look and behave very differently from the original elements.

Artists use charcoal to draw and sketch. Charcoal is a form of carbon.

AMAZING CARBON

You can find carbon anywhere on Earth. It is in charcoal and the lead in a pencil. Sparkling diamonds are pure carbon! Carbon also forms compounds with other elements, such as the carbon dioxide gas that animals produce by breathing.

PHYSICAL PROPERTIES OF CARBON

Each element is different. We can describe them by looking at their physical properties. An element's physical properties can be observed or measured without changing it into another substance.

DIFFERENT FORMS

Carbon can come in different forms, called allotropes. Diamond and graphite are allotropes of carbon. They are both made up purely of carbon atoms, but the atoms are arranged in different ways. The different arrangements give the allotropes different physical properties.

BUCKYBALLS

Another allotrope of carbon is buckminsterfullerene. In this form, molecules are made of 60 carbon atoms arranged in a spherical shape, like a soccer ball. They are often called "buckyballs."

LOOKING AT CARBON

We can use our senses to observe some of carbon's physical properties. Its color and odor are physical properties. So are its hardness and shininess. The temperature at which it melts or turns into a gas are physical properties, too.

HARDNESS: Diamond is one of the hardest substances we know. Graphite is much softer.

COLOR: Diamond is highly transparent, meaning see-through. Graphite is black, and you can't see through it.

BRITTLENESS: Carbon is very brittle, and cannot be rolled into wires or pounded into sheets.

Graphite and clay are mixed to make pencil cores.

CONDUCTIVITY: Graphite is a very good conductor of electricity. Diamond is not.

CHEMICAL PROPERTIES OF CARBON

We cannot tell an element's chemical properties by looking at it. Chemical properties affect how an element reacts with other substances.

CHEMICAL CHANGES

Elements react with other elements to make new substances, called compounds. The change is a chemical reaction. Carbon makes compounds with lots of other elements. Scientists have found more than 10 million compounds that contain carbon. A whole area of chemistry, called organic chemistry, studies carbon and its compounds.

Carbon dioxide gas is dissolved in soda and other soft drinks to give them their fizz.

Charcoal is mainly carbon. As it burns, it combines with oxygen.

HOW CARBON REACTS

Carbon forms so many different compounds that we know a lot about its chemical properties. Here are a few of them:

Carbon forms compounds with many other elements.

Carbon reacts with oxygen to form carbon dioxide (CO_2) or carbon monoxide (CO).

PHYSICAL OR CHEMICAL?

Water and ice are different forms of the same compound. Ice melts into water. This is a physical change. It can be easily reversed by putting the water in the freezer. But when carbon and oxygen react, they form a completely different substance: carbon dioxide. This is a chemical change. It is much harder to reverse.

As well as joining with other elements, carbon atoms can join to other carbon atoms. They make long chains or rings.

Carbon does not dissolve in water or acids.

WHERE IS CARBON FOUND?

Carbon can be found practically anywhere! Sometimes it exists in its pure form, but most of Earth's carbon is locked up in compounds with other elements.

HOW CARBON WAS DISCOVERED

Ancient people didn't realize that soot, graphite, and diamonds were all made of the same element. The French scientist Antoine Lavoisier named carbon, and in 1772 he proved that burning a diamond formed carbon dioxide. In 1796, the English chemist Smithson Tennant showed that diamonds were pure carbon.

Carbon is added to iron to make steel, which provides a strong framework for buildings and other structures.

The oceans take in carbon dioxide from the air. Sea creatures use it to make food or produce hard shells.

CARBON IN THE BODY

Your body is made up of trillions of tiny cells. Each one contains some carbon. Without carbon, there would be no you!

THE BIG FOUR

About 96 percent of the human body is made up of just four elements: oxygen, carbon, hydrogen, and nitrogen. Carbon is second on the list, making up 18 percent of your body's mass. There are actually more hydrogen atoms in the body than there are carbon atoms. But carbon atoms are much heavier, so they make up a larger proportion of the overall mass.

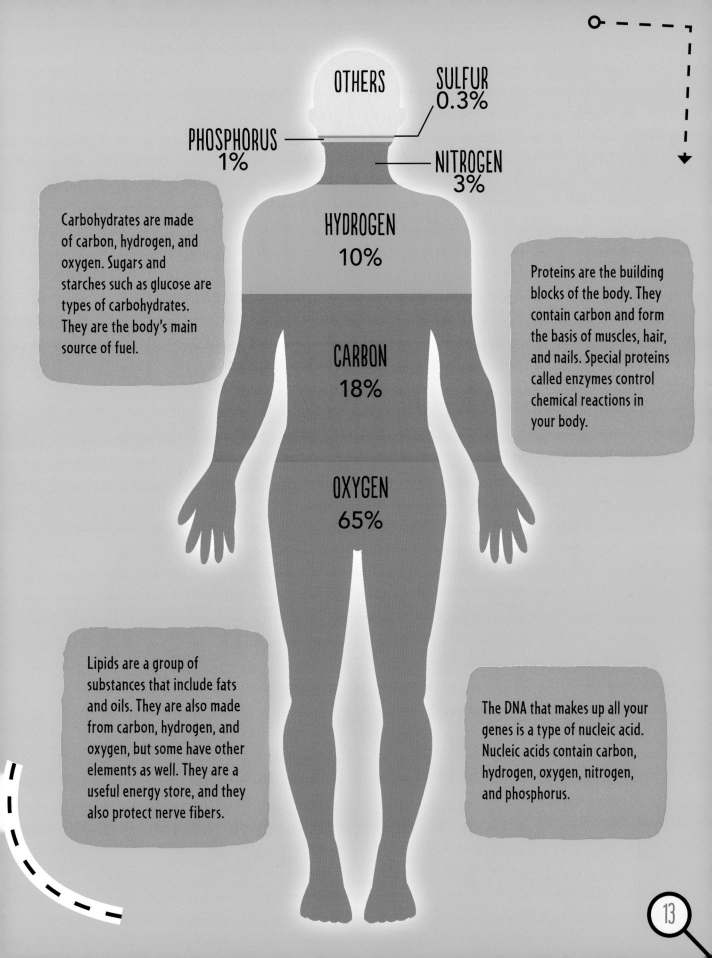

OTHERS

SULFUR
0.3%

PHOSPHORUS
1%

NITROGEN
3%

HYDROGEN
10%

CARBON
18%

OXYGEN
65%

Carbohydrates are made of carbon, hydrogen, and oxygen. Sugars and starches such as glucose are types of carbohydrates. They are the body's main source of fuel.

Proteins are the building blocks of the body. They contain carbon and form the basis of muscles, hair, and nails. Special proteins called enzymes control chemical reactions in your body.

Lipids are a group of substances that include fats and oils. They are also made from carbon, hydrogen, and oxygen, but some have other elements as well. They are a useful energy store, and they also protect nerve fibers.

The DNA that makes up all your genes is a type of nucleic acid. Nucleic acids contain carbon, hydrogen, oxygen, nitrogen, and phosphorus.

FUELING THE BODY

All the carbon in the human body has to come from somewhere. When you eat, you take in carbon.

CRUCIAL CARBOHYDRATES

Carbon bonds with hydrogen and oxygen to form carbohydrates—your body's main source of fuel. Eating foods that are rich in carbohydrates, such as fruits, vegetables, and grains, is how the body gets its carbon.

Fruits are a good source of simple carbohydrates.

Simple or Complex?

Carbohydrates can be simple or complex. Fruits and milk contain simple sugars. The body breaks them down quickly. The molecules in complex carbohydrates are made of longer chains of atoms. They take longer to break down. Beans and vegetables contain complex carbohydrates.

IN THE BODY

When you eat carbohydrates, your body breaks them down into simple sugars. The sugars are absorbed into the bloodstream. They travel all through the body and into individual cells. There, glucose combines with oxygen. This process releases energy. It also produces carbon dioxide and water as waste products.

When you exercise, you breathe hard. This takes more oxygen to your body's cells, allowing them to release more energy.

A BALANCED DIET

To stay healthy, your body needs more than just carbohydrates. It needs proteins and fats as well. They contain carbon, too!

CARBON AND PLANTS

Plants contain carbohydrates, but where did they come from? The answer is that instead of eating, plants make their own food. This amazing process is called photosynthesis.

PHOTOSYNTHESIS

Photosynthesis is almost the reverse of the way that humans release energy. Instead of breaking down sugars, plants create them. All they need is water, carbon dioxide, and energy in the form of sunlight. The sugars that plants produce are the ones that your body breaks down to use after you eat the plant.

Plants take in carbon dioxide from the air. It enters through tiny holes in the leaves.

Roots take in water from the soil. The water travels through the plant to the leaves.

Special compounds in the leaves absorb sunlight.

The energy from the sun allows a chemical reaction to happen. Water and carbon dioxide combine to form a simple sugar called glucose.

The plant can use the glucose right away, or store it to use later.

Leftover oxygen is released into the air.

Humans need oxygen to survive. We depend on the oxygen that trees and other plants release into the air.

COAL, OIL, AND GAS

A fuel is a substance that releases heat energy when it is burned. Some of the most important fuels we use today are coal, oil, and gas. They all contain carbon.

Butane is a hydrocarbon, with 4 carbon and 10 hydrogen atoms.

FOSSIL FUELS

We often call coal, oil, and gas "fossil fuels." This is because they are made from the remains of living things that died millions of years ago. Over time, their remains were buried by mud. This created great pressure, which combined with high temperatures to turn the dead organisms into fuel.

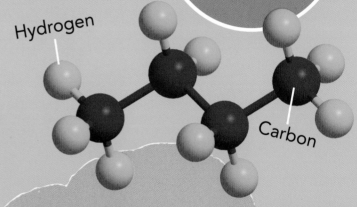

Hydrogen

Carbon

HYDROCARBONS

Coal, oil, and gas are hydrocarbons—compounds made up of carbon and hydrogen. These two elements can sometimes form long chains. Each "link" is a carbon atom bonded to two hydrogen atoms. There is another hydrogen atom at each end of the chain.

We must drill into the ground to find oil. Offshore oil rigs like this one dig under the ocean floor.

DIRTY FUELS

We burn fossil fuels to heat our homes and power our vehicles. We also use them in power stations to produce electricity. Burning fossil fuels releases carbon dioxide as well as energy. The carbon dioxide stays in the atmosphere, where it traps the sun's heat. Too much carbon dioxide in the air is making Earth's temperature rise.

THE CARBON CYCLE

Carbon is everywhere, but it doesn't always stay in one place. Carbon atoms circulate around the planet in a process called the carbon cycle.

Plants take in carbon dioxide from the air and make carbohydrates.

RECYCLING IS ELEMENTARY!

The amount of carbon on Earth is relatively constant. It is found in the ground, the air, and the oceans, as well as in living things. The carbon cycle allows all this carbon to get recycled.

Humans and animals eat plants, taking in the carbon compounds.

Humans and animals breathe out carbon dioxide.

Carbon dioxide dissolves in seawater and is stored in the oceans.

Volcanoes release carbon dioxide.

Fast or Slow?
A single carbon atom might pass from a plant to an animal to the atmosphere in just a few days. If it becomes part of a rock, it might stay trapped there for millions of years.

Burning coal and other fuels releases carbon dioxide into the air.

Living things called decomposers break down dead bodies and release carbon dioxide into the air.

Some plant and animal remains are buried underground. One day they may turn into fossil fuels.

Some sea creatures take in carbon from the water and use it to make shells.

Seashells may one day form a rock called limestone.

CARBON DATING

One feature of carbon is truly amazing. It can tell us how old things are! It's all thanks to a special form of carbon called carbon-14.

ISOTOPES

All atoms of a particular element have the same number of protons. The number of neutrons is often the same, but in some atoms it is different. These different forms are called isotopes. Carbon-12 and carbon-14 are isotopes of carbon.

DECAYING ELEMENTS

Nearly all carbon is a form called carbon-12, with 6 neutrons. Only about one in a trillion atoms is carbon-14, which has 8 neutrons. This substance will eventually lose particles and turn into nitrogen. After about 5,730 years, half of the carbon-14 atoms in an object will have turned into nitrogen. This process is called radioactive decay.

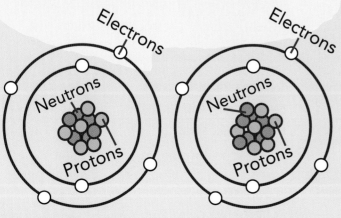

Carbon-12   Carbon-14

We can only use carbon dating on materials that were once alive, such as wood or bone.

THE CLOCK IS TICKING...

During its life, a living thing takes in a mixture of carbon-12 and carbon-14. But when it dies, it stops taking in carbon. The carbon-14 in its body will slowly decay, leaving only carbon-12. By measuring the ratio of carbon-12 to carbon-14, we can find out how long ago an object was alive.

USING CARBON

Carbon is one of the building blocks of our bodies, but it is useful in other ways, too. We use many carbon products in our everyday lives.

Pure iron is a fairly soft metal. Adding carbon to it forms steel, which is stronger and tougher. It is used in construction.

Tiny strands of carbon can be used to reinforce plastics, producing a material that is light and strong. This "carbon fiber" is used in bicycle frames, vehicles, sports equipment, and phone cases.

We turn coal, oil, and gas into plastics. These substances are lightweight, tough, and easy to mold into shape. Plastics are found everywhere, from packaging and toys to fabrics, cooking utensils, and light switches.

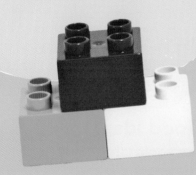

Graphite is pure carbon. It is in the "lead" in pencils. Graphite is also used as a lubricant in machines.

Tungsten carbide is a compound formed from carbon and an element called tungsten. It is very hard and strong. It is used in drill bits and cutting tools.

Carbon black is a powder. It is used to reinforce rubber in tires, and also as a pigment for coloring paints and printing inks.

THE PERIODIC TABLE

All the elements are organized into a chart called the periodic table. It groups together elements with similar properties. Each square gives information about a particular element.

A Good Idea!

The periodic table was developed in the 1860s by a Russian chemist named Dmitri Mendeleev. He left gaps that were later filled in with new elements, as they were discovered.

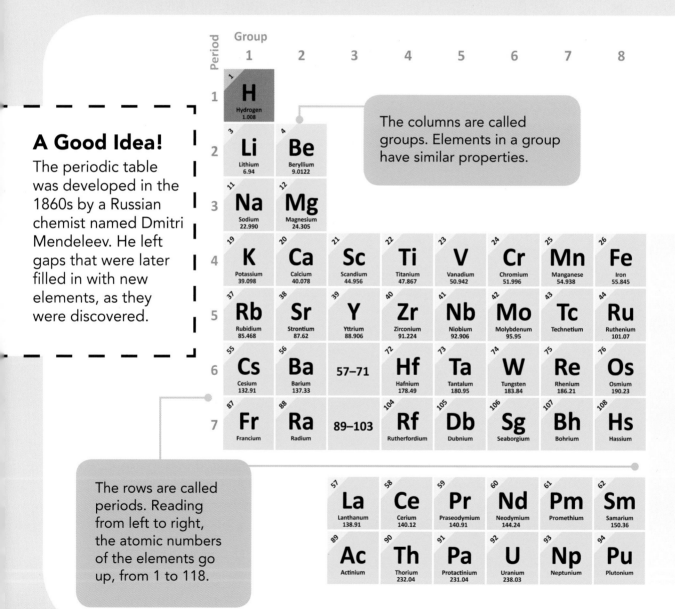

The columns are called groups. Elements in a group have similar properties.

The rows are called periods. Reading from left to right, the atomic numbers of the elements go up, from 1 to 118.

Every element has an atomic number. It shows how many protons are in each of its atoms. Carbon's atomic number is 6.

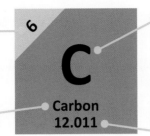

6

C

Carbon
12.011

The chemical symbol is one or two letters, often an abbreviation of the element's name. It is the same in all languages.

Each square shows the element's name. Different languages use different names.

A number shows the element's atomic weight. It is an average of the number of protons and neutrons in the different isotopes of an element.

9	10	11	12	13	14	15	16	17	18

Metalloids (semimetals)

Non–metals

Metals

2
He
Helium
4.0026

5
B
Boron
10.81

6
C
Carbon
12.011

7
N
Nitrogen
14.007

8
O
Oxygen
15.999

9
F
Fluorine
18.998

10
Ne
Neon
20.180

13
Al
Aluminum
26.982

14
Si
Silicon
28.085

15
P
Phosphorus
30.974

16
S
Sulfur
32.06

17
Cl
Chlorine
35.45

18
Ar
Argon
39.948

27
Co
Cobalt
58.933

28
Ni
Nickel
58.693

29
Cu
Copper
63.546

30
Zn
Zinc
65.38

31
Ga
Gallium
69.723

32
Ge
Germanium
72.630

33
As
Arsenic
74.922

34
Se
Selenium
78.971

35
Br
Bromine
79.904

36
Kr
Krypton
83.798

45
Rh
Rhodium
102.91

46
Pd
Palladium
106.42

47
Ag
Silver
107.87

48
Cd
Cadmium
112.41

49
In
Indium
114.82

50
Sn
Tin
118.71

51
Sb
Antimony
121.76

52
Te
Tellurium
127.60

53
I
Iodine
126.90

54
Xe
Xenon
131.29

77
Ir
Iridium
192.22

78
Pt
Platinum
195.08

79
Au
Gold
196.97

80
Hg
Mercury
200.59

81
Tl
Thallium
204.38

82
Pb
Lead
207.2

83
Bi
Bismuth
208.98

84
Po
Polonium

85
At
Astatine

86
Rn
Radon

109
Mt
Meitnerium

110
Ds
Darmstadtium

111
Rg
Roentgenium

112
Cn
Copernicium

113
Nh
Nihonium

114
Fl
Flerovium

115
Mc
Moscovium

116
Lv
Livermorium

117
Ts
Tennessine

118
Og
Oganesson

63
Eu
Europium
151.96

64
Gd
Gadolinium
157.25

65
Tb
Terbium
158.93

66
Dy
Dysprosium
162.50

67
Ho
Holmium
164.93

68
Er
Erbium
167.26

69
Tm
Thulium
168.93

70
Yb
Ytterbium
173.05

71
Lu
Lutetium
174.97

Lanthanide elements

95
Am
Americium

96
Cm
Curium

97
Bk
Berkelium

98
Cf
Californium

99
Es
Einsteinium

100
Fm
Fermium

101
Md
Mendelevium

102
No
Nobelium

103
Lr
Lawrencium

Actinide elements

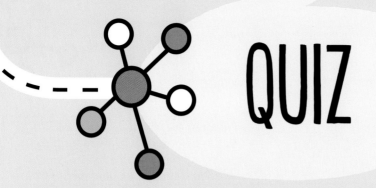

QUIZ

Try this quiz and test your knowledge of carbon and elements! The answers are on page 32.

1

What makes elements unique?

a. their groovy sense of style
b. they cannot be broken down into other substances
c. they are only found on Earth

2

Why are diamond and graphite so different?

a. diamonds are made of glass and graphite is made of lead
b. diamonds are just frozen graphite
c. their atoms are arranged in different ways

3

What do you get when you combine carbon and oxygen?

a. helium
b. either carbon dioxide or carbon monoxide
c. a headache

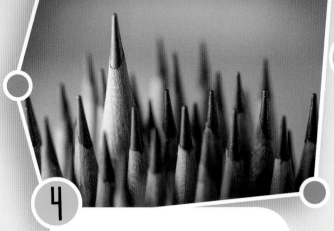

5

What do plants need to make their own food?

a. a good recipe and a ride to the grocery store
b. oxygen and hydrogen
c. water, carbon dioxide, and sunlight

4

How much of your body is made up of carbon?

a. about 18 percent
b. the top half
c. just the hair and nails

6

Why are coal, oil, and gas called "fossil fuels"?

a. they are made from the remains of plants and animals
b. they were invented a long time ago
c. only dinosaurs use them

7

What type of carbon is used for carbon dating?

a. carbon-12
b. carbon-14
c. carbon fiber

8

What happens to the carbon dioxide that we breathe out?

a. it goes into the atmosphere
b. it turns into diamonds
c. it freezes into snowflakes

GLOSSARY

allotropes different forms of the same element. Allotropes of an element have the atoms arranged in different patterns.

atmosphere the layers of gases that surround the earth

atom the smallest possible unit of a chemical element. Atoms are the basis of all matter in the universe.

bond to form a link with other atoms, either of the same element or of a different element

carbohydrates compounds such as sugars and starches, which are made from carbon, hydrogen, and oxygen

carbon dioxide gas found in the air that plants need to survive

cell the smallest unit of life. All plants and animals are made of cells.

chemical change change that occurs when one substance reacts with another to form a new substance

chemical property characteristic of a material that can be observed during or after a chemical reaction

compound substance made of two or more different elements bonded together

electron a tiny particle with a negative charge that moves outside the nucleus of an atom

element a substance that cannot be broken down or separated into other substances

energy the ability to do work. Energy can take many different forms.

fossil fuels fuels such as oil, coal, and gas, which are formed from the decaying remains of living things

fuel anything that can be burned as a source of energy, such as wood or gasoline

gas form of matter that is neither liquid or solid. "Gas" can also refer to natural gas found in Earth's surface and used as a fuel.

hydrocarbons compounds made up of carbon and hydrogen atoms

isotopes different forms of the same element that have different numbers of neutrons

liquid form of matter that is neither a solid nor a gas, and flows when it is poured

lubricant substance that stops the moving parts in a machine from rubbing against each other

mass the total amount of matter in an object or space

molecule the smallest unit of a substance that has all the properties of that substance. A molecule can be made up of a single atom, or a group of atoms

neutron a particle in the nucleus of an atom

nucleus the center of an atom

oxygen gas found in the air that living things need in order to survive

photosynthesis the process by which a plant uses sunlight to change water and carbon dioxide into food

physical property characteristic of a material that can be observed without changing the material

proton a positively charged particle in the nucleus of an atom

react to undergo a chemical change when combined with another substance

FURTHER RESOURCES

BOOKS

Arbuthnott, Gill. *Your Guide to the Periodic Table.* New York, NY: Crabtree Publishing Company, 2016.

Belton, Blair. *How Coal Is Formed.* New York, NY: Gareth Stevens Publishing, 2017.

Callery, Sean, and Miranda Smith. *Periodic Table.* New York, NY: Scholastic Nonfiction, 2017.

Dakers, Diane. *The Carbon Cycle.* New York, NY: Crabtree Publishing Company, 2015.

Dickmann, Nancy. *Burning Out: Energy from Fossil Fuels.* New York, NY: Crabtree Publishing Company, 2016.

McKinney, Donna B. *Carbon (Exploring the Elements).* New York, NY: Enslow Publishing, 2019.

WEBSITES

Here is a website with facts about fossil fuels: **climatekids.nasa.gov/carbon/**

Go here for more detail on the carbon cycle: **earthobservatory.nasa.gov/Features/CarbonCycle/**

Learn about all the elements using this interactive periodic table: **www.rsc.org/periodic-table/**

Learn more about carbon in your body: **youngzine.org/news/science/why-all-life-carbon-based**

INDEX

Quiz answers
1. b; 2. c; 3. b; 4. a; 5. c; 6. a; 7. b; 8. a